AQA GCSE

Physics
Required Practicals
Exam Practice Workbook

Primrose Kitten

T0347618

OXFORD
UNIVERSITY PRESS

Contents

Introduction

As part of your AQA GCSE Physics course, you will carry out ten Required Practicals. You can be asked about any aspect of any of these during the exams; this can include planning an investigation, making predictions, taking readings from equipment, analysing results, identifying patterns, drawing graphs, or suggesting improvements to the method. You can also be asked about practicals that are similar but that you may not have done before. You need to be able to recognise and apply the key practical skills that you have learnt to different experiments.

These practical questions account for at least 15% of the total marks. This Exam Practice Workbook allows you to practise answering questions on the ten Required Practicals and become familiar with the types of questions you may find in the exams. There are lots of hints and tips about what to look out for when answering practical questions. Answers to all questions are available at oxfordsecondary.co.uk/required-practicals-answers.

Practical method – Full details of all ten Required Practicals, including equipment, method, and safety information, will remind you of the practical work you have carried out and the important skills you have gained during the course

Exam tips – Hints on how you can approach the practical exam questions, improve your answers, and secure marks

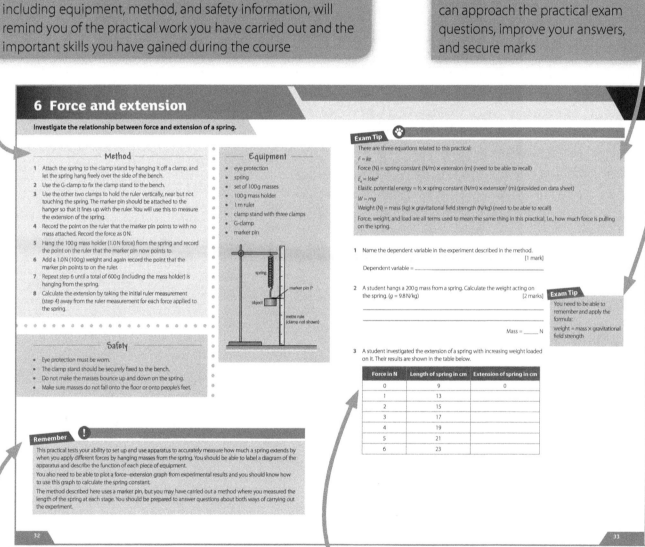

Remember – Each practical has a reminder of the key skills being tested in the practical, whatever the context

Exam-style questions – Lots of practical exam-style questions about each Required Practical help you to become confident in answering practical questions

1 Specific heat capacity

Determine the specific heat capacity of a material.

Method

1 Check the mass of the block of material you are using (it may be written on the block, or your teacher will be able to tell you).

2 The block should be wrapped securely in insulation and placed on an insulating mat.

3 With the power supply switched off, set up the apparatus as shown in the diagram.

4 Place the thermometer in the block and measure the temperature. Record this as the 'starting temperature' of the block.

5 Switch the power supply on and start the stopwatch.

6 Record the current and potential difference.

7 Watch the reading on the thermometer. Record the temperature every 60 seconds for ten minutes.

8 When the temperature reaches 15°C above the starting temperature, switch off the power supply and stop the stopwatch.

9 Record the thermometer reading and the time on the stopwatch.

Note: The thermometer reading might continue to increase for up to a few minutes after the heater has been switched off. Measure and record the highest reading of the thermometer after the heater was switched off.

Equipment

- 12V, 24W low-voltage heater
- 12V power supply for heater
- ammeter and voltmeter
- two connecting leads
- aluminium block with holes for a heater and a thermometer
- insulation for block (including a thick insulating mat to place under it)
- rubber bands or tape to fix insulation around block

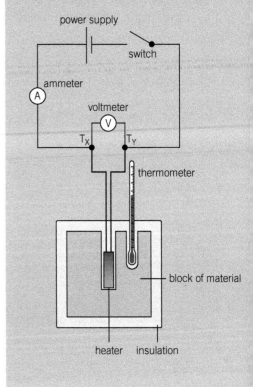

Safety

- Do not touch electrical equipment, plugs, or sockets with wet hands.
- Do not touch the heater: it becomes very hot when in use, and can stay hot for a long time after it is switched off.
- Switch the heater off if you think it is overheating.
- Always switch the heater off when you are not using it.
- When the thermometer is not being used, make sure it is placed where it cannot easily roll off the table.

Remember

This practical tests whether you can find out the specific heat capacity of a material by measuring current, potential difference, time and temperature. You should be able to describe the method, including details of how to use your results and any calculations you need to do.

Remember that a graph of temperature against work done should produce a straight line and the gradient of this line can be used to calculate the specific heat capacity.

1   The equation below can be used to calculate the energy transferred in joules into the block of metal in a certain number of seconds.

Energy (J) = power x time (s)

Give the unit of power in this equation.   **[1 mark]**

Unit of power = _____

2   As part of this experiment you needed to set up a circuit including an ammeter and a voltmeter.

Tick the **two** correct statements that describe how they should be set up.

                                                  [2 marks]

An ammeter should be connected in series   ☐

An ammeter should be connected in parallel   ☐

A voltmeter should be connected in series   ☐

A voltmeter should be connected in parallel   ☐

3   Two students investigated the specific heat capacity of identical blocks. Student A insulated their block with polystyrene. Student B did not use any insulation.

Explain which student's results would be more accurate.   **[4 marks]**

_____

_____

_____

_____

_____

_____

_____

_____

5

4   A student investigated the specific heat capacity of bronze. They measured
    how many seconds it took for the temperature of the block to increase by 1°C.
    Explain how the student could make their measurement more accurate.

Exam Tip

Remember that the command word 'explain' means you need to give reasons in your answer.

                                                                    [2 marks]

_____

_____

_____

_____

5   A student uses a stopwatch that shows the time in minutes and seconds.
    Convert 3 minutes 15 seconds into seconds.   [1 mark]

_____

_____

                            Answer = _____ s

6   Define specific heat capacity.   [1 mark]

_____

_____

_____

7   Specific heat capacity can be found using the following equation:

$$\text{specific heat capacity} = \frac{\text{energy transferred}}{\text{mass} \times \text{temperature change}}$$

    Rearrange the equation so it could be used to find the temperature change.
                                                                    [2 marks]

8   The above equation refers to energy transferred but when a graph is drawn for
    this experiment we use work done instead of energy transferred.
    work done = force × distance.
    Using this information, give 5 J in Nm.   [1 mark]

Hint

Think about what the units for force and distance are.

_____

_____

9 Explain why the hole where the thermometer is placed is filled with water.

[2 marks]

_____

_____

_____

_____

10 In this practical you used a thermometer and took a reading every minute to follow the temperature change. An alternative would be to use a temperature probe with a data-logger.

a Give two advantages of using a data-logger. [2 marks]

_____

_____

_____

b Suggest a disadvantage of using a data-logger. [1 mark]

_____

11 a 1 kg blocks of copper, steel, and aluminium are heated with the same power.

Use the data in the table to explain which block's temperature will take the most time to increase by 30°C. [2 marks]

Metal	Specific heat capacity in J/kg °C
copper	385
steel	452
aluminium	913

_____

_____

_____

b A student carried investigated the specific heat capacity of an unknown metal. They recorded the following data.

Time in s	Temperature in °C	Work done in kJ
0	21	0
60	22	1.8
180	28	5.4
300	36	9
420	44	12.6
540	52	16.2
600	56	18

Hint

The data for work done is given in kJ in the table. The standard unit for work done is J. You have to draw your graph in kJ but make sure that you use J when you do the calculation.

i On the axes provided below:

- plot these results
- draw a line of best fit. [3 marks]

Hint

The specific heat capacity can be found from the gradient of the **straight** section of the graph. You can then compare this with the data in **11a** to find the closest match.

Exam Tip

Always use the largest triangle you can draw to get an accurate gradient, and remember:

$$\text{gradient} = \frac{\text{change in up } (y)}{\text{change in across } (x)}$$

ii Use the data table in part **a** and your graph to determine the identity of the metal. [1 mark]

_____

_____

c The student who recorded the data in part **b** has not recorded the data for work done correctly.

Describe how the data should have been recorded and explain why this change is important. [2 marks]

_____

_____

_____

_____

Hint

It's not the units.

12 A student draws a graph of their results and notices that the first part of the graph is curved. This curve is followed by a straight section.

Suggest why the first part is curved. [2 marks]

_____

_____

_____

_____

13 Ⓗ A student carried out the same experiment with a block of copper of unknown mass.

Use the data below to calculate the mass of the block.

Give you answer to an appropriate number of significant figures.   [6 marks]

Current in circuit = 1.2 A

Potential difference in the circuit = 12 V

Temperature change at 4 minutes = 8°C

_____

_____

_____

_____

_____

_____

_____

_____

_____

_____

Answer = _____ kg

Hint

You'll need to use all the equations in the 'key points'. To keep things simple, you'll need to use them in the order they are given.

Not all of the data is given in standard units so you'll need to do some converting before you start calculating.

Exam Tip

Sometimes you might need to look at earlier parts of a question to find the information you need. For example, the specific heat capacity for copper is given is **11a**.

2 Thermal insulation

Investigate the effectiveness of different types and thicknesses of materials as thermal insulators.

Method

A Investigating different types of material

1. Set up your containers. Leave one container unwrapped. Wrap each of the other containers in a different material using elastic bands or tape to hold the material in place. Try to use the same thickness of each material.

2. Prepare lids for the containers from the same material as the wrapping if possible, or else made of aluminium foil or cling film.

3. Make a hole in each lid which is just big enough for a thermometer to fit through.

4. Use the measuring cylinder to pour equal amounts of hot water into each container.

5. Put the lids onto the containers with a thermometer fitted through each lid so that it rests near the bottom of the water.

6. Start the stopwatch and measure the starting temperature of the water.

7. Every three minutes for 15 minutes, use the thermometer to gently stir the water and then measure and record the temperature of the water in each beaker.

B Investigating different thicknesses of a material

8. Choose one material from those you used in experiment **A**.

9. Again, leave one container unwrapped and wrap each of the other containers in different numbers of layers of the chosen material.

10. Repeat steps 2–7.

Equipment

- four identical containers (beakers, boiling tubes, or metal cans)
- measuring cylinder
- four thermometers
- stopwatch
- insulating materials to test
- elastic bands or tape
- aluminium foil or cling film (if needed for lids)

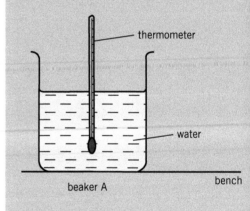

beaker A

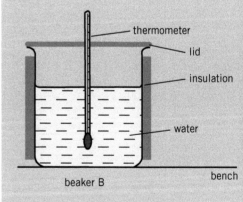

beaker B

Safety

- Wear eye protection in case the hot water splashes.
- Take care when transporting or pouring hot water. If you need to move hot water from one place to another, warn everyone nearby before you walk through.

Remember

There are two different experiments in this practical. You should be able to describe the methods for each of them in detail.

This practical is testing your ability to make and record measurements of time, volume, and temperature in order to measure energy transfers.

This practical could be linked to equations that you may not expect to appear into this section.

$E = mc\Delta\theta$

energy transferred = mass × specific heat capacity × temperature change

       (J)   (kg)   (J/kg °C)   (°C)

This equation is given to you in the exam, but you need to be confident in your ability to apply it.

1 **a** Describe what happens to that thermal energy lost from the water in this practical. [1 mark]

_____

_____

b Give the function of each of the following pieces of equipment in this practical.

   i Lid [1 mark]

_____

   ii Measuring cylinder [1 mark]

_____

   iii Thermometer [1 mark]

_____

Every piece of equipment in each practical has a function. It's a good idea to make sure you know why each piece of equipment is important.

c Describe **two** advantages of using a data logger instead of a thermometer. [2 marks]

_____

_____

_____

d Complete the following paragraph using the words in the box below. [4 marks]

| bar chart | categoric | continuous | control | dependent |
| independent | line graph | sketch graph | | |

Student A wants to draw a graph of temperature against time. They should

plot a _____ because their data is _____.

Student B wants to plot a graph of temperature change against the

type of material. They should plot a _____ because their

_____ variable is _____ data.

2 The temperature of 0.80 kg of water was measured as it cooled.

The starting temperature of the water was 84 °C and the temperature after five minutes was 61 °C.

The specific heat capacity of water is 4.2 J/kg °C

a Calculate the energy transferred over the five minute period and give the units in your answer. [3 marks]

_____

_____

_____

Energy transferred = _____

b Calculate the percentage change in the temperature of the water over the five minute period. [2 marks]

_____

_____

_____

Answer = _____%

Hint

Don't forget to make your answer negative if the value has decreased.

3 Student A and B wrapped their beakers in four layers of bubble wrap.

Student B popped all of the bubbles on their bubble wrap before using it.

Both students had the same volume of water and the water was at the same temperature.

Predict the results you would expect and explain your prediction. [4 marks]

_____

_____

_____

_____

_____

_____

4 A student carried out an experiment testing how effective cardboard was as a thermal insulator. Their data is shown below.

Time in minutes	Temperature in °C
0	90
10	65
20	46
30	33
40	26
50	24

a   Plot the student's data on the axes provided.   [4 marks]

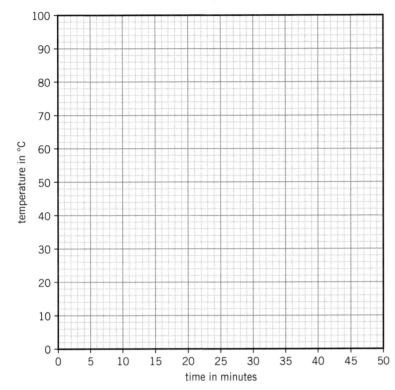

b   Describe the shape of the graph.   [3 marks]

_____

_____

_____

_____

_____

c   Estimate the rate of heat loss at 25 minutes.   [3 marks]

Exam Tip

If you are asked to estimate a rate from a curved graph, you will need to draw a tangent and then calculate the gradient.

Answer = _____ °C/min

5 Two students investigated the effectiveness of several materials as thermal insulators. Their results are shown below.

Time in minutes	Temperature in °C			
	No insulation	Newspaper	Bubble wrap	Cotton wool
0	89	72	92	68
5	81	65	86	64
10	74	58	80	60
15	67	62	75	56
20	61	46	71	53
25	56	41	66	50
30	51	36	62	47

Student A concludes that the bubble wrap was the best thermal insulator. Student B concludes that the cotton wool was the best thermal insulator.

a Evaluate the two students' conclusions. [4 marks]

Exam Tip

This is a question about analysis of data, so you should quote data in your answer!

_____

_____

_____

_____

_____

_____

_____

_____

b Suggest what modifications the students could make to make the results easier to compare. [2 marks]

_____

_____

_____

6 A student investigated the rate of cooling of water in an insulated coffee cup. After one hour, the student immediately calculated the rate of cooling but then lost the piece of paper where they recorded the final temperature.

Calculate the temperature of the water after one hour. [3 marks]

Room temperature in °C	Starting temperature in °C	Average rate of cooling (over one hour) in °C/min	Final temperature (after one hour) in °C
25	65	0.9	

Hint

Make sure you've used all the data given.

7 A housing developer wants to carry out an experiment to help them choose the best thermal insulating material to use when building energy efficient houses. The available materials are:

- air
- expanding foam
- polystyrene beads
- wool fibre.

a Explain why it important to build energy efficient houses. [3 marks]

_____

_____

_____

_____

b Give **two** advantages of using models. [2 marks]

_____

_____

c Write a plan for an experiment that could be used as a model to investigate the effectiveness of the four materials. [6 marks]

_____

_____

_____

_____

_____

_____

_____

_____

_____

_____

_____

_____

_____

_____

_____

Exam Tip

This question is set in a slightly different context to the original investigation, but the science behind it is exactly the same. If you are asked to write a plan or describe a method, it will usually be very similar to the one you carried out in class – you just have to apply what you know to the context given.

3 Resistance

Investigate factors that affect resistance in electrical circuits.

Method

A The effect of the length of a wire on resistance

1   Set up the apparatus as shown in Figure 1.

2   Set the length of the test wire to 100 cm by adjusting the positions of the crocodile clips.

3   Turn the power supply on at 1.5 V and close the switch.

4   Record the readings of voltage and current.

5   Repeat steps 2 to 4, decreasing the length of the test wire by 10 cm each time to a minimum of 20 cm.

B Resistance in series and parallel circuits

1   Set up two resistors in series as shown in Figure 2a.

2   Close the switch and record readings of voltage and current for the series circuit.

3   Set up the two resistors in parallel as shown in Figure 2b.

4   Close the switch and record readings of voltage and current for the parallel circuit.

Equipment

- piece of wire to test
- low-voltage power supply or batteries
- switch
- connecting leads
- crocodile clips
- metre ruler
- ammeter and voltmeter
- wire-wound resistors

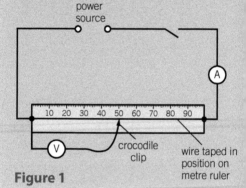

Figure 1

Safety

- Do not connect the wire directly to the mains supply – this could cause a fatal electric shock.
- Do not let the current get higher than 1.0 A. Use a variable resistor to keep the current low if necessary.
- Disconnect the circuit as soon as the measurements are taken, to stop the wire getting hot.
- After the circuit has been on, do not touch the wire without checking first whether you can feel heat coming off it from a distance, using the back of your hand.

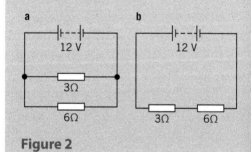

Figure 2

Remember

There are two separate experiments in this practical. One investigates how resistance across different lengths of wire varies. The other investigates how the arrangement of resistors in series and parallel circuits affects the resistance in the circuit. You should understand and be able to describe how to accurately measure current, potential difference, and resistance in both experiments.

As part of this practical, you are expected to be able plot and interpret a graph of resistance against length.

For a series circuit the total resistance in a circuit is the sum of all the resistors. Make sure you learn the equation:

$R_{total} = R_1 + R_2 + R_3 \dots$

You need to know and be able to apply the equation:

potential difference = current × resistance

1   Use the words in the box below to complete the following sentences.

[2 marks]

| ammeter | current | potential difference | voltmeter |

In this experiment, the _____ measures the _____ flowing through the circuit.

The _____ measures the _____ across the resistor.

2   A student set up the following circuit.

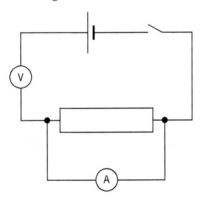

a   Identify the error the student has made in setting up the equipment.

[1 mark]

_____

_____

b   When the student corrects the error, the ammeter and voltmeter both read zero.

Suggest what they need to change to be able to take readings.   [1 mark]

_____

c   When the student gets the circuit working the ammeter reads 0.50 A and the voltmeter reads 0.75 V.

Calculate the resistance of the resistor and choose the correct units from the box below.   [3 marks]

| A | Ω | V | R | I |

_____

_____

_____

Resistance = _____ units = _____

3

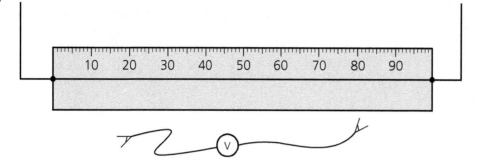

a A student wants to record the resistance across a 0.2 m length of wire.

On the diagram above, draw an X at each point where the student should clip the crocodile clips that are attached to the voltmeter. [1 mark]

Hint

Make sure you remember to convert the units.

b A 'zero error' is often seen in this experiment.

Describe a potential source of a zero error in this experiment. [2 marks]

_____

_____

_____

c Sketch a graph on the axes provided to show the results you would predict in this experiment. [1 mark]

Exam Tip

When the command word is 'sketch', you only need to draw a line to show the overall shape of the graph. You don't need to plot any individual points.

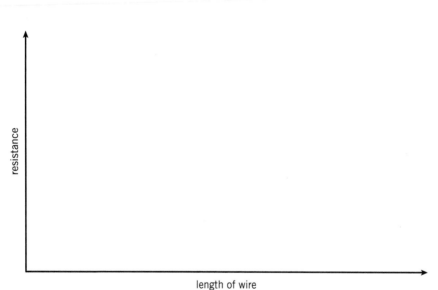

4 A student investigated the effect of the length of a wire on its resistance. The student repeated their experiment three times. Their results are shown below.

Length of wire in cm	Resistance in ohms			
	Test 1	Test 2	Test 3	Mean
20	4.02	4.10	4.62	
40	8.24	8.36	8.97	
60	12.60	15.67	12.98	
80	16.13	16.27	16.84	
100	19.04	19.25	19.99	

a Circle the anomalous result in the table.   [1 mark]

b Calculate the mean for each length of wire to complete the table.
                                                                      [3 marks]

c The student did not allow the wire to cool down between each repeat experiment.
   Explain the effect this had on the repeatability of the student's results.
                                                                      [3 marks]

_____

_____

_____

_____

_____

Exam Tip

Remember not to include any anomalous results when calculating a mean.

Hint

You should quote examples from the results in your answer.

d • Use the data in the table to plot a graph of mean resistance in ohms against length of wire in cm.
   • Draw a line of best fit.   [4 marks]

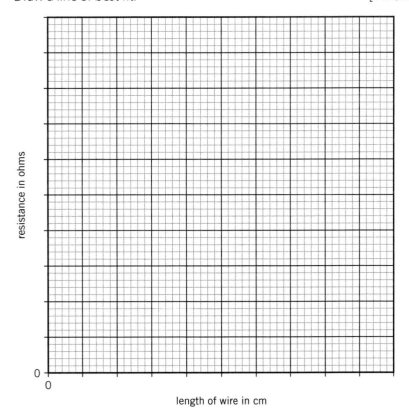

resistance in ohms

length of wire in cm

5 a In another experiment the length of the wire was kept constant and the cross-sectional area of the wire was changed.

Predict the effect that doubling the cross-sectional area of the wire would have on the resistance of the wire. [1 mark]

_____

_____

_____

_____

b A variable resistor is often used in this experiment to keep the current below 1.0 A.

Explain why the resistance of a wire will increase if the circuit is left on for a long time with a high current flowing. [4 marks]

Exam Tip

This is an 'explain' question, so it wants you to give reasons why something happens.

_____

_____

_____

_____

_____

_____

6 The diagrams below show the two components arranged in series and in parallel.

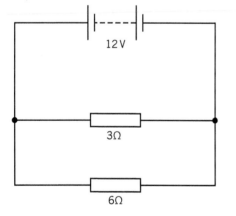

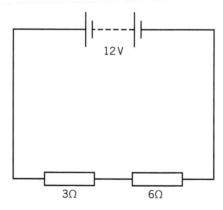

a Calculate the total resistance in the series circuit. [1 mark]

_____

_____

_____

Total resistance = _____ Ω

b Explain why the resistance in the parallel circuit will be lower than the value calculated in part **a**. [3 marks]

_____

_____

_____

_____

_____

_____

Hint

This question is really just asking you to explain the difference between resistance in parallel and series circuits.

7 **H** A circuit was set up and left on for 3 minutes. During this time the energy in the circuit was recorded as 45 J and the charge was 9 C.
Calculate the resistance in the circuit. [4 marks]

_____

_____

_____

_____

_____

_____

_____

_____

_____

_____

_____

Resistance = _____ Ω

4 I–V characteristics

Investigate the effect of potential difference across a component on the current flowing through it.

Method

1 With the power supply switched off, set up the circuit shown in Figure 1.

2 You will adjust the variable resistor and measure the current and potential difference for your component. Do not allow the current to go above 1.0 A.

3 Starting with the variable resistor at its lowest resistance (so that the current is at its highest), measure the current and potential difference for your component.

4 Switch off the power supply.

5 Increase the resistance of the variable resistor in about six steps between the minimum and maximum resistances, and each time measure the current and potential difference for the component. Switch off the power supply between readings.

6 Reverse the polarity of the power pack by swapping the positive and negative connections and repeat steps 1-5.

7 Repeat the experiment for each component you are testing. When testing a diode, you should insert a fixed resistor in series with the diode, and swap the ammeter for a milliammeter.

Equipment

- power supply or battery pack
- components to test:
  - diode
  - filament lamp
  - resistor
- variable resistor
- ammeter
- voltmeter
- connecting leads

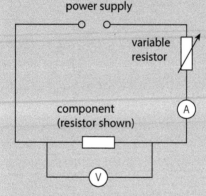

Figure 1

Safety

- Components may get hot after being on for a while, so you should not touch them.
- Do not allow the current to go above 1.0 A, as this could cause overheating.
- Always switch off the power supply or disconnect the batteries before building or changing your circuit, and switch off the power supply between measurements.

 Remember

This experiment compares the way the current flowing through a component changes when the potential difference across that component is varied. The skills being tested are your ability to accurately measure current and potential difference, and whether you can understand and draw circuit diagrams. The results can be plotted on a graph of current (I) against potential difference (V). The particular shape of each I–V graph is described as the characteristic of the component.

Exam Tip

Filament bulbs, resistors, and diodes all have unique *I–V* characteristics. You should be able to recognise or sketch each component's *I–V* graph. You will also need to be able to explain their shape. You need to remember this equation for the resistance practical, but it is really important here as well:

$$\text{resistance}\ (\Omega) = \frac{\text{potential difference}\ (V)}{\text{current}\ (A)}$$

1 Draw one line from each circuit symbol to its name. [4 marks]

Battery

Cell

 Diode

Filament lamp

 Thermistor

Variable resistor

2 a i Sketch the current–potential difference graph for a filament lamp.
[3 marks]

Exam Tip

When 'sketch' is the command word, you need to show the axes, the shape of the graph, and any coordinates where the line crosses the axes (if relevant). Sometimes the axes will be provided. You don't need a scale on the axes in a sketch graph.

ii Explain the shape of the current–potential difference graph for a filament lamp. [4 marks]

_____

_____

_____

_____

_____

_____

3 A student investigates the *I–V* characteristics of two unknown components. Their results are shown below.

Potential difference in V	Current in A Component 1	Current in A Component 2
−3.0	−0.14	0.00
−2.0	−0.12	0.00
−1.0	−0.05	0.00
0.0	0.00	0.00
1.0	0.05	0.01
2.0	0.11	0.18
3.0	0.15	0.40

a Plot both sets of data on the axes provided below. [4 marks]

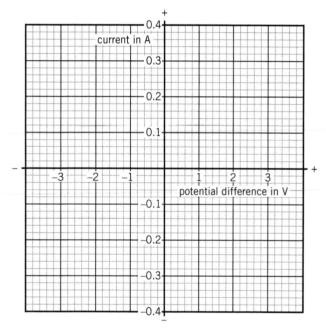

b Identify the components the student was testing. [2 marks]

- Component 1 = _____

- Component 2 = _____

c Compare and explain the shapes of the current–potential difference graphs for the two components. [6 marks]

_____

_____

_____

_____

_____

_____

_____

_____

d Use the graph to predict the current through component 1 when the potential difference across it is 4.0 V. [1 mark]

_____

_____

Current = _____ A

e Use the graph for component 1 to find its resistance. [3 marks]

_____

_____

Resistance of component 1 = _____ Ω

4 A student carried out two tests on a resistor with a fixed value. Their results are recorded below.

	Test 1	Test 2
current in A	14.8	9.2
potential difference in V	7.4	

Hint

You don't need to know the resistance to be able to answer this question – it's simply ratios.

a Use the values for test 1 to calculate the value of the resistor. [1 mark]

_____

_____

Resistance = _____ Ω

b Complete the table with the final measurement of potential difference. [2 marks]

_____

_____

_____

5 Explain why *I–V* characteristics always go through the origin. [2 marks]

_____

_____

6 In this experiment, describe the purpose of reversing the battery. [2 marks]

_____

_____

7 Suggest an advantage of using a milliammeter instead of an ammeter. [1 mark]

_____

_____

5 Density

Investigate the density of regular- and irregular-shaped solids and liquids.

Method

A Density of a solid (in the shape of a cube or cuboid)

1 Measure and record the mass of the solid.

2 Measure and record the length, width, and height of the solid.

B Density of a solid (irregular-shaped sample)

3 Measure and record the mass of the sample.

4 Fill a measuring cylinder half-full with water. (There needs to be enough water so that when you put the solid into the water, the water will cover the solid but will not rise above the top of the measuring scale.)

5 With your eye level with the water's surface, measure the volume of water and record it.

6 Carefully place the solid material into the container.

7 Measure and record the new volume of the water.

C Density of a liquid

8 In your table for liquids, write the type of liquid whose density you are measuring.

9 Measure and record the mass of an empty measuring cylinder.

10 Pour the liquid into the measuring cylinder, making sure it does not go above the top of the cylinder's measuring scale.

11 Measure and record the mass of the cylinder with the liquid in it.

12 Measure and record the volume of liquid in the cylinder.

Equipment

- regular-shaped solid material
- irregular-shaped solid material
- liquid in a regular-shaped container
- balance
- ruler (30 cm is long enough)
- measuring cylinder

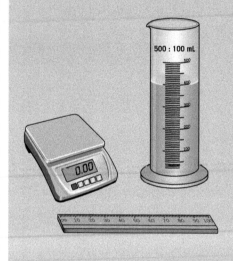

Safety

- Clean up any water spills straight away, reduce the risk of slipping.

Remember !

There are three separate experiments in this practical. You should be able to describe the methods for all three. This practical tests your ability to make accurate measurements of dimensions, mass, and volumes.

1   Draw one line from each object to the most appropriate set of equipment
    needed to safely find its density.   [3 marks]

| Pebble |

| Balance and a measuring cylinder |

| Textbook |

| Balance and a ruler |

| Battery |

2   When an object is placed into a displacement can, water pours out.
    Describe what the volume of water is equal to.   [1 mark]

    _____

    _____

3   Suggest why it is important that an object is completely submerged before
    you measure the volume of water displaced.   [1 mark]

    _____

    _____

4   A block of clay is found to have a volume of $50\,cm^3$ and a mass of $65\,g$.

    a   Write the equation that links density, mass, and volume   [1 mark]

    b   Calculate the density of the block.   [2 marks]

    _____

    _____

    _____

                    Density of clay block = _____ kg/m^3

5 a Calculate the volume of a 0.5 m³ cube in cm³. [2 marks]

_____

_____

Volume of block = _____ cm³

Hint

The answer is not 50 cm³. Remember that this is a three-dimensional shape!

b The block in part **a** has a density of 4.2 g/cm³.

Calculate the mass of the block in kg. [3 marks]

_____

_____

Mass of block = _____ kg

6 Give two possible sources of error in this experiment. [2 marks]

_____

_____

7 100 ml of water has a mass of 100 g.

60 ml of honey has a mass of 87 g.

Identify which liquid is denser. [3 marks]

_____

_____

_____

_____

_____

_____

Answer = _____

Exam Tip

If there is data in the question, always try to use it in your answer.

8 A chess piece is carved from a regular cylinder of wood with a diameter of 4 cm and a height of 5 cm.

a Calculate the volume of the cylinder (use π = 3.14). [2 marks]

_____

_____

_____

Volume of cylinder = _____ cm³

Hint

Volume of a cylinder = $\pi r^2 h$

b Describe how you could use the apparatus pictured below to find out how much wood has been removed from the cylinder when carving the chess piece. [6 marks]

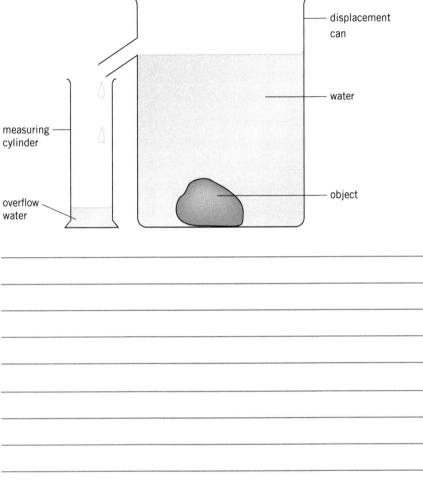

measuring cylinder

overflow water

displacement can

water

object

_____

_____

_____

_____

_____

_____

_____

_____

_____

_____

_____

c A student weighs the cylinder before and after it was carved. Its mass was 44 g before carving and 33 g after it was carved.

Estimate the volume of the chess piece. [3 marks]

> **Hint**
>
> This question just needs you to use ratios to work out the answer. You will need your answer from part **a**.

_____

_____

_____

_____

Volume of finished chess piece = _____ cm³

9 An irregular-shaped object has a recorded mass of 5.47 g.

The displays of three balances are shown below.

A	B	C
000.0 g	00.00 g	0.000 g

a Choose the balance which would be most appropriate to check the accuracy of the recorded mass. Tick **one** box. [1 mark]

A ☐

B ☐

C ☐

b Justify your answer to part **a**. [2 marks]

_____

_____

_____

> **Hint**
> You may need to say why the other two balances are not as appropriate as your choice.

10 A student wants to identify an unknown liquid chemical in a bottle. Table 1 shows data the student recorded. Table 2 shows the densities of some common liquids.

Table 1

Mass of empty measuring cylinder	64.6 g
Mass of measuring cylinder with unknown liquid	142.8 g
Volume of unknown liquid	85 cm³

Table 2

Liquid	Density g/cm³
acetone	0.79
olive oil	0.92
petroleum	0.69
turpentine	0.87
water	1.00

Determine which of the liquids in Table 2 is most likely to be the unknown sample. [3 marks]

_____

_____

_____

_____

_____

Unknown sample = _____

11 A student heats some ice cubes in a beaker using a Bunsen burner. Describe the changes in the density of the water in terms of mass and volume.

[3 marks]

_____

_____

_____

_____

_____

Exam Tip

If you really understand the equations in physics. They can tell you a lot of information that can be used to answer longer written questions as well as maths questions.

12 The density of water is 1000 kg/m³.

Object A has a density of 492 kg/m³.

Object B has a density of 3673 kg/m³.

Explain what will happen to objects A and B when they are placed in a beaker of water.   [3 marks]

_____

_____

_____

_____

_____

_____

13 Calculate the mass of an object that has a density of 9300 kg/m³, a depth of 20 cm, a height of 15 cm and a width of 42 cm.   [3 marks]

_____

_____

_____

_____

_____

_____

Mass of object = _____ kg

6 Force and extension

Investigate the relationship between force and extension of a spring.

Method

1 Attach the spring to the clamp stand by hanging it off a clamp, and let the spring hang freely over the side of the bench.

2 Use the G-clamp to fix the clamp stand to the bench.

3 Use the other two clamps to hold the ruler vertically, near but not touching the spring. The marker pin should be attached to the hanger so that it lines up with the ruler. You will use this to measure the extension of the spring.

4 Record the point on the ruler that the marker pin points to with no mass attached. Record the force as 0 N.

5 Hang the 100 g mass holder (1.0 N force) from the spring and record the point on the ruler that the marker pin now points to.

6 Add a 1.0 N (100 g) weight and again record the point that the marker pin points to on the ruler.

7 Repeat step 6 until a total of 600 g (including the mass holder) is hanging from the spring.

8 Calculate the extension by taking the initial ruler measurement (step 4) away from the ruler measurement for each force applied to the spring.

Equipment

- eye protection
- spring
- set of 100 g masses
- 100 g mass holder
- 1 m ruler
- clamp stand with three clamps
- G-clamp
- marker pin

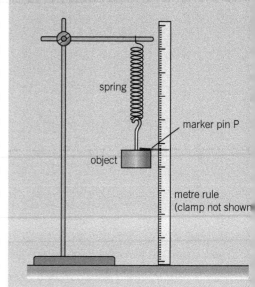

spring

marker pin P

object

metre rule
(clamp not shown)

Safety

- Eye protection must be worn.
- The clamp stand should be securely fixed to the bench.
- Do not make the masses bounce up and down on the spring.
- Make sure masses do not fall onto the floor or onto people's feet.

Remember !

This practical tests your ability to set up and use apparatus to accurately measure how much a spring extends by when you apply different forces by hanging masses from the spring. You should be able to label a diagram of the apparatus and describe the function of each piece of equipment.

You also need to be able to plot a force–extension graph from experimental results and you should know how to use this graph to calculate the spring constant.

The method described here uses a marker pin, but you may have carried out a method where you measured the length of the spring at each stage. You should be prepared to answer questions about both ways of carrying out the experiment.

1 Name the dependent variable in the experiment described in the method.

[1 mark]

Dependent variable = _____

2 A student hangs a 200 g mass from a spring. Calculate the weight acting on the spring. ($g = 9.8$ N/kg) [2 marks]

_____

_____

Mass = _____ N

3 A student investigated the extension of a spring with increasing weight loaded on it. Their results are shown in the table below.

Force in N	Length of spring in cm	Extension of spring in cm
0	9	0
1	13	
2	15	
3	17	
4	19	
5	21	
6	23	

a Complete the table. [1 mark]

b • Plot the data on the axes provided below.

• Draw a line of best fit. [3 marks]

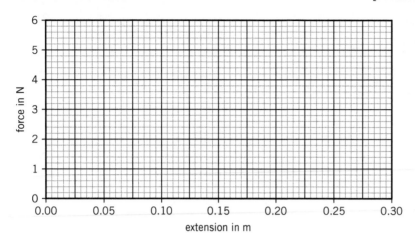

c Use the graph to name the type of relationship between weight and spring extension. [1 mark]

_____

_____

d Predict what might happen to the shape of the graph if more weight was added. [3 marks]

_____

_____

_____

_____

_____

_____

e Calculate the percentage change in length of a spring loaded with 6 N compared to an unstretched spring. [3 marks]

_____

_____

_____

% change in length = _____ %

f Use the graph to calculate the spring constant. [3 marks]

_____

_____

_____

_____

Sprint constant = _____ N/m

4 Suggest why it is important that safety glasses are worn in this practical.

[1 mark]

_____

_____

5 Describe the function of the 'pointer' in this experiment. [1 mark]

_____

_____

6 Look at the diagram below.

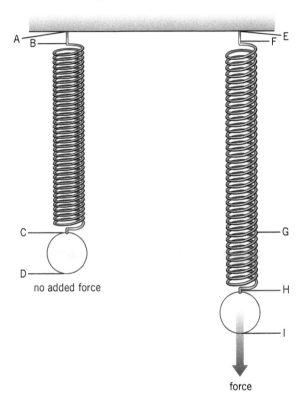

force

a Identify which points the initial length of the spring should be measured between.

Tick **one** box. [1 mark]

A and C ☐   B and C ☐

A and D ☐   B and D ☐

b Choose which points the length of the extended spring should be measured between. [1 mark]

Answer = _____ and _____

c   Two students realise that they have measured all their lengths between the wrong two points (E and I).

- Student A says this will affect the accuracy of their results.
- Student B thinks that it will affect the precision of their results.

Explain which student is correct.   [3 marks]

_____

_____

_____

_____

_____

Exam Tip

You are being asked to explain and the question is worth three marks. This means you need to pick the correct student, give a reason why they are right, and possibly a reason why the other student is wrong.

7   A student carried out this experiment to compare the extension of two different springs.

One spring was very stiff and the other was easy to extend.

Describe the differences you would expect in the graphs force (x-axis) against extension (y-axis) for these two springs.   [2 marks]

Exam Tip

You can use a sketch graph to aid you answer if you wish, but make sure you add helpful labels or annotations.

_____

_____

_____

_____

_____

8   A trampoline manufacturer is investigating the spring constant of one of their trampoline springs by increasing the force pulling it and measuring the extended length.

a   Explain why it is better to measure the length of the whole spring than just measuring the extension of the spring directly.   [2 marks]

_____

_____

_____

b   Describe the changes in energy stores as weight is applied to the spring.
                                                            [1 mark]

_____

_____

c   The graph below shows the results of the manufacturer's experiment.

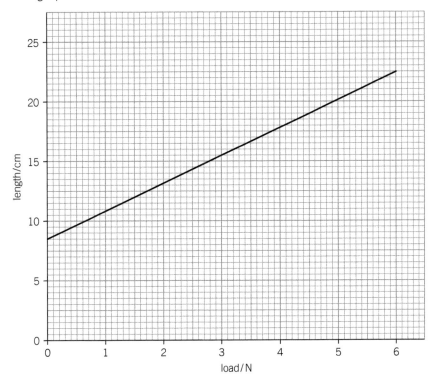

Describe the steps you would take to calculate the mass that would produce and extension of 5 cm.   [3 marks]

_____

_____

_____

_____

_____

_____

_____

7 Acceleration

Investigate the relationship between force, mass, and acceleration.

Method

A The effect of force on the acceleration of a constant mass

1 Set up the apparatus as shown in Figure 1, with five chalk lines at 20 cm intervals. The distance from the start point to the edge of the bench should be 100 cm.

2 Check that the string is parallel to the bench.

3 Load the mass holder with 100 g and hold the trolley at the start point.

4 Set the stopwatch to lap mode.

5 Release the trolley at the same moment as starting the stopwatch.

6 Press the lap timer each time the trolley passes one of the chalk marks.

7 Record the times in a table.

8 Repeat steps 5 to 7 for masses of 80 g, 60 g, 40 g, and 20 g. To keep the mass of the system constant, you should stick the masses you remove from the holder on the trolley.

B The effect of an object's mass on its acceleration

9 Use the results of experiment A to choose a suitable weight to accelerate the trolley. Load the hanger with this mass.

10 Stick 100 g of masses on the trolley using the sticky tape.

11 Repeat steps 4-7 of experiment A.

12 Repeat steps 10 and 11 another five times increasing the mass by 100 g each time.

Equipment

- trolley
- ruler
- sticky tape
- chalk
- pulley with clamp
- mass holders
- 50 g masses
- 100 g masses
- string or strong thread

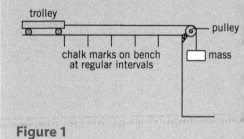

Figure 1

Safety

- The pulley must be safely attached to the bench.
- Masses should be securely attached to the trolley.
- Make sure no one is standing where the mass holder or masses could land on their feet.
- Make sure the trolley does not fall off the table.

Remember !

You investigated whether the amount of force pulling an object changed its acceleration. You also investigated whether the mass of the trolley affected its acceleration when the force applied was kept constant.

Remember that this practical is testing your ability to observe the effect of a force by making and recording measurements of length, mass, and time. You should know how to use these measurements to calculate speed and acceleration.

1   Use words from the box below to complete Newton's second law.   [3 marks]

acceleration	energy	forces	mass	speed	weight

An object's _____ depends on the _____ acting on the object and the _____ of the object.

2   A student was testing how force affected the acceleration of a trolley with a mass of 800 g.

Calculate the force acting on the trolley when the acceleration was 5 m/s².
[2 marks]

_____

_____

_____

Force acting on trolley = _____ N

3   Two students carried out this experiment.
    • Student A used the apparatus in Figure 1.
    • Student B used the apparatus in the diagram below.

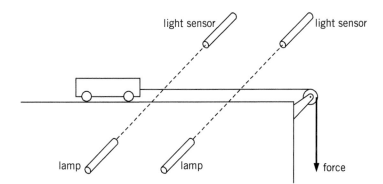

a   Evaluate the two students' methods.   [4 marks]

_____

_____

_____

_____

_____

_____

3 b Give a potential source of error in student A's method and suggest how they could record more accurate data without using light gates.   [2 marks]

_____

_____

_____

_____

c What is the function of the pulley this experiment?   [1 mark]

Tick **one** box.

Control direction of the trolley   ☐

Prevent the trolley falling off   ☐

Protect feet   ☐

Reduce friction   ☐

4 A student drew a graph of their data. The trolley used had a mass of 1.25 kg.

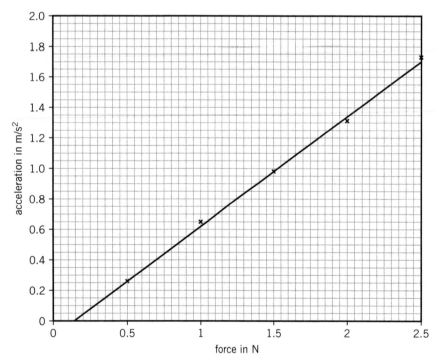

a Calculate the theoretical acceleration if the force is 1.5 N.   [1 mark]

_____

_____

Acceleration = _____ m/s²

b The student observed that the line of best fit doesn't go through the origin and the values they measured were always lower than the calculated theoretical acceleration.

Explain the student's observations. [3 marks]

_____

_____

_____

_____

_____

5 Draw a free-body diagram to show the forces acting on the trolley in this practical. [4 marks]

6 There are a number of forces acting upon the object in this practical. Classify the following forces as either contact or non-contact forces. [5 marks]

friction	gravity	air resistance	push	pull

Contact force	Non-contact force

7 Describe the difference between speed and velocity. [2 marks]

_____

_____

_____

_____

8   A group of students tested how acceleration was affected by changing the force acting on a trolley of constant mass.

Force in N	Acceleration in m/s²
2	0.98
4	1.92
6	2.93
8	3.92
10	4.70

a   Plot the data on the axes provided.   [3 marks]

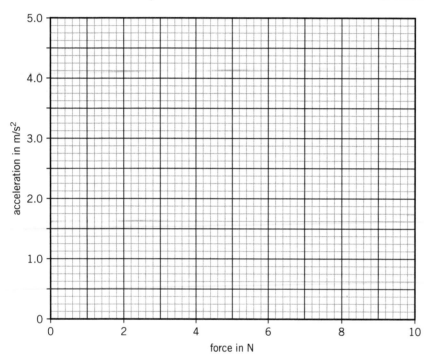

b   Describe the type of relationship seen in the graph.   [1 mark]

_____

_____

Another student changed the mass but kept a constant force acting on the car.

Mass of car in kg	Acceleration in m/s²
2	4.92
4	2.46
6	1.64
8	1.23
10	0.99

c   Use the data to estimate a value for the resultant force accelerating the car.   [2 marks]

_____

_____

_____

Resultant force = _____ N

9 An accelerating trolley of mass 1.5 kg passed one light gate with a velocity of 4.5 m/s.

The trolley passed a second light gate 3 seconds later with a velocity of 5.1 m/s. Calculate the resultant force acting on the trolley. [4 marks]

_____

_____

_____

_____

Resultant force = _____ N

10 A student uses a single light gate to record the velocity of a trolley 30.0 cm from its starting position. The trolley begins at rest and the velocity is recorded as 3.87 m/s. The equation for uniform acceleration is:

$$v^2 - u^2 = 2as.$$

a Rearrange the equation to make a the subject of the formula. [1 mark]

> **Exam Tip**
>
> This equation is given in the Physics equation sheet in the exam, but you need to know how to apply it.
>
> Remember that s means distance – not speed!

b Calculate the acceleration of the trolley. [2 marks]

_____

_____

_____

_____

Acceleration of trolley = _____ m/s²

c The trolley has a mass of 200 g.

Estimate the mass of the hanger that is pulling on the trolley.

(g = 9.8 N/kg) [5 marks]

_____

_____

_____

_____

Mass of hanger = _____ g

8 Waves

Investigate the behaviour of waves in solids and liquids.

Method

A Wave behaviour in a solid

1 Assemble the apparatus as shown in Figure 1.

2 Measure the length of string between the vibration generator and the pulley.

3 Turn on the signal generator.

4 Increase the frequency of the vibration from zero until you can see one complete wave on the string.

5 Record the frequency of the signal generator.

6 Continue to increase the frequency until you see a second wave pattern, with two complete waves.

7 Record the frequency on the signal generator.

8 Continue this process to find the frequencies which form three and four complete waves on the string.

B Wave behaviour in a liquid

1 Set up the ripple tank as shown in Figure 2.

2 Fill the tray with water about 1 cm deep. The dipper should just touch the surface of the water.

3 Place the lamp so that it shines into the tray.

4 Turn on the power supply and lower the speed until separate waves are clearly visible on the screen below.

5 Measure the distance between the two furthest apart visible waves on the screen. Divide this distance by the number of waves visible to calculate the wavelength.

6 Count the number of waves passing a fixed point over a period of 10 seconds. Divide this number by ten to find the frequency.

Equipment

- signal generator
- oscillator
- masses on a mass holder
- length of string
- tape measure
- ripple-tank
- low-voltage power supply
- lamp

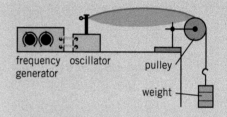

Figure 1

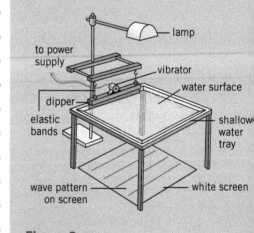

Figure 2

Safety

- Do not touch the vibration generator when it is in motion.
- Be careful not to drop masses on the floor.
- Clean up any water spill immediately.
- If using a lamp, keep the lamp as far away from the water as possible.
- Do not touch the lamp or electrical supply with wet hands.

Remember

This practical tests your ability to use information from very different types of equipment to investigate the properties of waves in solids and in liquids. The physics and the theories are the same in both experiments – they both allow speed, frequency, and wavelength to be measured.

1 Figure 1 shows the apparatus for investigating the behaviour of a wave on a string.

    a Sketch the wave produced on the string and label it with the amplitude and the wavelength.   **[3 marks]**

    b Describe the direction of movement of particles and transfer of energy in the wave on the string.   **[2 marks]**

_____

_____

_____

2 A student pushes a slinky back and forth to investigate longitudinal waves.
Use the words provided to label the diagram of the student's experiment.
      [3 marks]

compression   rarefaction   wavelength

direction of travel

3 When using a ripple tank, the wave may travel very quickly making it difficult
to measure the wavelength.

Setting up a strobe light can make the wave appear stationary and make them
easier to count and measure.

a Suggest an alternative way to measure the wavelength accurately that
does not involve a strobe light. [3 marks]

_____

_____

_____

_____

b Explain the function of the white screen and the lamp. [2 marks]

_____

_____

_____

c Using the ripple tank, a student counted 22 waves passing a fixed point in
5.0 seconds.

Calculate the frequency of the waves in the ripple tank. [2 marks]

Frequency of waves = _____ Hz

d The student measured the wavelength of the waves in part b to be 0.03 m.
Calculate the wave speed and select the correct units from the box below.
[4 marks]

| Hz | m | m/s | m/s^2 | s |

_____

_____

_____

Wave speed = _____ Units = _____

4 The diagram below shows what a student observed when investigating a wave on a string.

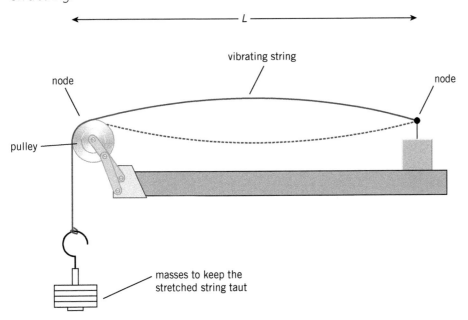

The student made the following claim.

'Wavelength can't be measured as there isn't a full wave on the string.'

Explain whether the student is correct. [3 marks]

_____

_____

_____

_____

5 Two students carried out an experiment measuring waves in a ripple tank.
   • Student A measured the wavelength of a single wave.
   • Student B measured the wavelength of ten waves and then divided the value by 10.

Explain which student's data will be the most accurate and why. [3 marks]

_____

_____

_____

_____

6 Give an advantage of using a wave generator or a motor to produce waves in a ripple tank, instead of producing them by hand. [1 mark]

_____

7 A student carried out a version of the ripple tank experiment to investigate waves radiating out in a circle. A diagram of their experiment is shown below.

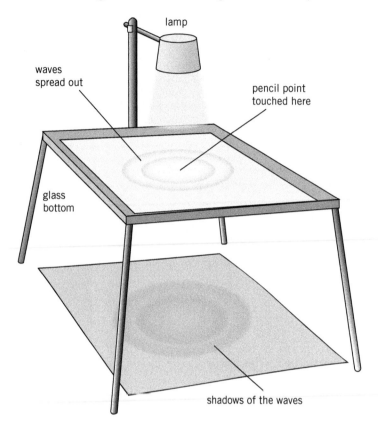

lamp

waves spread out

pencil point touched here

glass bottom

shadows of the waves

Exam Tip

This is a slightly different experiment because the waves are forming circles rather than straight lines. Don't be put off by the slight difference – the theory is exactly the same!

a Describe how the student should use this apparatus to estimate the wave speed as accurately as possible. [6 marks]

_____

_____

_____

_____

_____

_____

_____

_____

_____

_____

_____

_____

_____

_____

b The student counted 17 waves passing a fixed point in 11 seconds.
Calculate the frequency of the waves. [3 marks]

_____

_____

_____

Frequency = _____ Hz

Exam Tip

There is often a mark for giving your answer to the correct number of significant figures. Remember that you should never give more significant figures than the original numbers in the question.

8 A scientist is investigating the properties of an electromagnetic wave in a vacuum. Their detector measures the frequency, f as 2.0×10^{10} kHz. The speed of electromagnetic waves in a vacuum is 3.0×10^8 m/s.
Calculate the wavelength of the electromagnetic wave. [3 marks]

_____

_____

_____

_____

_____

Wavelength = _____ m

Hint

Pay close attention to the units given to you in the question. Do you need to convert anything?

9 Light

Use different substances and surfaces to investigate the refraction and reflection of light

Method

1 Place the glass block in the centre of the piece of paper (landscape view) and draw around its edges.

2 Remove the block and draw a dotted normal line at right angles to the edge of one long side of the block, about halfway along.

3 Draw a line to represent the incident ray at 30° to the normal.

4 Place the block back on the rectangle you have drawn.

5 Switch on the ray box with a narrow slit in front of the bulb and shine the ray along the incident ray you have drawn.

6 Observe the path of the light through the block and out of the other side.

7 Mark the path of the emergent light ray on the other side with a pencil line. Also mark any reflected ray you can see.

8 Remove the glass block. Draw a normal at the point where the light emerged from the glass block.

9 Draw a line to join the incident and emergent ray through the rectangle representing the glass block to give the refracted ray.

10 Your drawing should now look like this diagram. Measure the angles shown in the diagram using the protractor and record your results.

11 Repeat for an angle of incidence of 50°.

Equipment

- glass block and Perspex block
- ray box, narrow slit, power supply
- sheet of plain white paper
- pencil, ruler, and rubber
- protractor
- other transparent materials

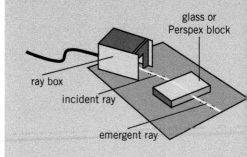

Safety

- Take care with the ray box because the lamp will become hot.
- Check the glass or Perspex block does not have any sharp edges before use.
- Be careful not to drop glass or Perspex blocks.

Remember !

The skills being tested in this practical are your ability to observe the effect of electromagnetic waves interacting with different materials. You should be able to describe the method in detail and understand the function of each piece of equipment.

1 A student carries out the experiment described in the method. Their drawing is shown below.

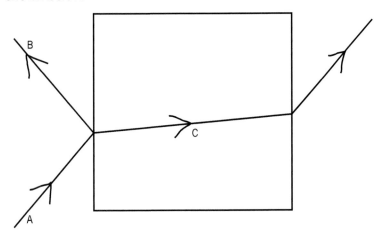

a Draw **two** lines to show where the student should draw the normals.

[2 marks]

b Three rays are labelled **A, B,** and **C**.

Draw **one** line from each letter to the correct name of the ray. [3 marks]

Letter   **Name of ray**

Critical

A   Incident

B   Normal

C   Reflected

Refracted

c Describe **two** possible sources of error in this experiment. [2 marks]

_____

_____

_____

d Describe what would happen to the beam of light if it hit the block at an angle of 90° to the surface. [2 marks]

_____

_____

2 A student directed a beam of white light through a prism using the set up shown below.

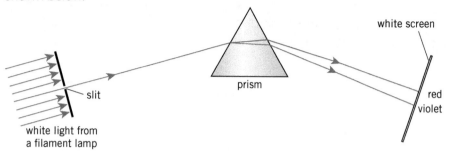

They observed a rainbow effect on the white screen, with all the colours of the visible spectrum.

a Fill in the gaps to complete the order of colours the student observed.

[3 marks]

red
violet

b Complete the paragraph below using words from the box.　　　[5 marks]

frequency　　longitudinal　　reflection　　refraction
speed　　transverse　　wavelength

All colours of visible light have the same _____ and are all

_____ waves. A prism separates white light into the bands of

the visible spectrum because each band has a different _____

and _____. This means that the angle of _____ is

different for each colour of visible light.

c Suggest an alternative type of wave that could be used to investigate reflection or refraction.　　　[1 mark]

_____

3 A student was comparing refraction in two different materials. They measured the angles with the ray pointing at three different points on each block. Their results are shown below.

Glass	
Angle of incidence in degrees	Angle of refraction in degrees
47	30
38	24
29	18

Perspex	
Angle of incidence in degrees	Angle of refraction in degrees
62	36
52	31
43	26

a Give an advantage of measuring the angles of incident and refraction at three different points on the surface of each block. [1 mark]

_____

_____

b The student's teacher says they should have kept the angle of incidence the same for all six tests.

Give **two** advantages of using the same angle of incidence for each test. [2 marks]

_____

_____

_____

_____

c Suggest whether light travels slower in glass or Perspex and explain your answer using data from the table. [3 marks]

_____

_____

_____

_____

_____

4   **a**   A student was investigating reflection of light at the plane of a mirror. They positioned the ray box so that the angle of incidence was 65°.

Draw an accurate diagram of their results.   [5 marks]

    b   The student then carried out an experiment to investigate refraction.

They positioned the ray box so that the angle of incidence was 35° and found that the angle of refraction was 22°.

Draw an accurate diagram to show their results.   [5 marks]

5   Describe what happens to a ray of light when the critical angle is exceeded.

    [2 marks]

_____

_____

_____

6 Instead of carrying out this experiment in the laboratory, this practical can also be carried out as a computer simulation.

Evaluate the use of simulations in physics. [6 marks]

_____

_____

_____

_____

_____

_____

_____

_____

_____

_____

_____

Exam Tip

In an evaluate question, you need to consider evidence for and against something, give you opinion, and justify your opinion. It usually doesn't matter what your opinion is – as long as it is based on the advantages and disadvantages and you justify it.

Sometimes a planning table can help you structure a balanced answer.

For	Against

7 a Describe what happens to a beam of light when it is refracted. [2 marks]

_____

_____

_____

_____

b Explain why light is refracted [5 marks]

_____

_____

_____

_____

_____

_____

_____

_____

_____

Exam Tip

Pay close attention to the differences in what each part of question 7 is asking you. Remember that 'describe' means you should say what is happening. 'Explain' means you need to say why something is happening.

c Describe what determines how much a ray of light is refracted when it passes through the boundary between two materials. [1 mark]

_____

_____

Investigate the amount of infrared radiated from different types of surfaces.

Method

A Emission of infrared radiation by silver and black cans.

1 Place the two drinks cans on a heatproof mat. Beakers with aluminium foil lids can be used as an alternative.

2 Carefully pour 150 ml of hot water into each of the two cans using a measuring cylinder.

3 If you are using beakers, place the lids onto the beakers.

4 Put a thermometer into the water in each container.

5 Start the stopwatch, and record the temperature of the water in the two containers every 30 s for 10 minutes.

B Emission of infrared radiation from a Leslie cube.

1 Place the Leslie cube on a heatproof mat and fill it with hot water.

2 Use an infrared thermometer/detector to measure the amount of infrared radiating from one surface of the Leslie cube.

3 Carefully rotate the Leslie cube to measure the amount of infrared radiating from each of the surfaces.

4 Record your results in a suitable table.

Make sure the infrared detector/thermometer is always the same distance from the surface being tested.

Equipment

- two drink cans (one painted silver and one painted matt black)
- two thermometers
- measuring cylinder
- stopwatch
- hot water
- heatproof mat
- heatproof gloves
- Leslie cube
- infrared thermometer or detector

thermometer to measure water temperature at intervals as it cools

painted silver   painted matt black

Safety

- Wear eye protection in case of hot water splashes.
- Take care with hot water. Use heatproof gloves if you need to move hot water from one place to another and warn anyone that is nearby before you move.
- Clean up any water spills straightaway.
- Do not touch the hot water containers, as they will get very hot. Leave them to cool before clearing them away after the practical.

Remember !

This practical is all about investigating how the type of surface affects the amount of infrared radiation that is emitted. There are lot of different methods for this practical. Some methods involve fancy equipment and others use very basic equipment. The science behind the experiment is the same no matter how you carried out the practical.

Applying your knowledge to unfamiliar situations is an important skill for you to practice as exam questions will usually try to present information in a way you haven't seen before. Try to work out how what you see relates to the experiment that you did.

1 a Complete the order of waves in the electromagnetic spectrum using the terms in the box below. [2 marks]

| x-rays | ultraviolet | infrared | microwaves |

radio waves
visible light
gamma rays

b On the electromagnetic spectrum you completed in part **a**, circle the type of radiation that is emitted by hot objects. [1 mark]

c State the main source of this radiation on Earth. [1 mark]

_____

d List two properties all electromagnetic waves have in common. [2 marks]

_____

_____

2 A student investigates the emission of radiation from a silver can and a matt black can as described in the method section.

a Describe three variables that should be controlled in this experiment.

[3 marks]

_____

_____

_____

_____

The student's results are shown below.

Time in seconds	Temperature of water in °C	
	Silver can	Matt-black can
0	98	98
60	90	85
120	83	74
180	75	64
240	68	55
300	62	49

b   Use the results to identify which can is the better emitter of infrared
    radiation and give a reason for your choice.   [2 marks]

_____

_____

_____

c   Calculate the rate of temperature change for each can in °C/s.   [4 marks]

_____

_____

_____

_____

_____

_____

Rate of temperature change for silver can = _____ °C/s

Rate of temperature change for matt-black can = _____ °C/s

d   Calculate the % change in the temperature of the water in the silver can
    between 0 seconds and 300 seconds.   [2 marks]

_____

_____

_____

% change in the temperature of the water in silver can = _____ %

e The student also has an infrared lamp available.

Describe how the student would use this equipment to investigate which can is the best absorber of infrared radiation. [6 marks]

_____

_____

_____

_____

_____

_____

_____

_____

_____

3 A student wants to investigate how the temperature of water in a can affects the amount of infrared radiated.

a Circle the correct options to complete the student's hypothesis below.

[4 marks]

'I predict that the amount of **infrared/ultraviolet** radiation
emitted/absorbed by the can will be **directly/inversely** proportional
to the temperature of the water in the can.

This is because the **higher/lower** the temperature of an object,
the more infrared radiation it emits.'

b Sketch a graph on the axes below to show the results that the hypothesis predicts. [2 marks]

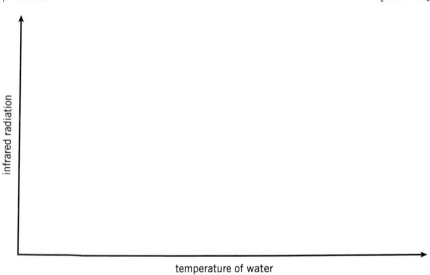

infrared radiation

temperature of water

4 A student plans an experiment to measure the amount of infrared radiation emitted from different surfaces using the apparatus shown below.

[1 mark]

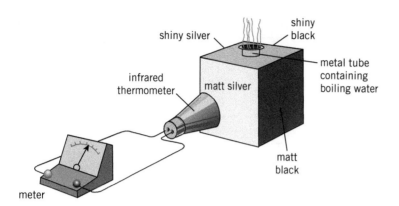

a Name the independent variable in this experiment. [1 mark]

_____

_____

Exam Tip

Time is precious in an exam so do NOT start you answer, 'in this experiment the independent variable is....'
Repeating the question won't gain you any marks – just give the answer.

A student measured the infrared radiation from the four different surfaces using the infrared detector.

Surface	Infrared radiation in units
shiny silver	17
matt silver	35
shiny black	39
matt black	47

Exam Tip

Some tables and graphs have variables that say 'in units' or 'in arbitrary units'. If you see this in an exam don't panic – they are just used to show a general trend or values when the actual units are not needed.

b Plot this data on the graph paper provided below. [4 marks]

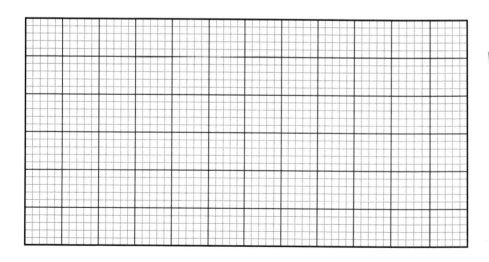

Exam Tip

Think carefully about the type of graph you draw when one of the variables is categoric data.

c   The student's hypothesis was:

'The colour of the surface will affect emission of infrared radiation more than the roughness of the surface.'

Write a conclusion based on the student's results and their hypothesis.

[4 marks]

_____

_____

_____

_____

_____

_____

Exam Tip

If you are asked to write a conclusion, always quote data to back up what you are saying.

d   Predict which surface would be the best absorber and which surface would be the poorest absorber of infrared radiation and explain why in each case.

[4 marks]

_____

_____

_____

_____

_____

_____

Hint

You could draw an annotated diagram to help answer this question.

Physics equations

You should be able to remember and apply the following equations, using SI units, for your assessments.

Word equation	Symbol equation
weight = mass × gravitational field strength	$W = mg$
force applied to a spring = spring constant × extension	$F = ke$
acceleration = $\dfrac{\text{change in velocity}}{\text{time taken}}$	$a = \dfrac{\Delta v}{t}$
Ⓗ momentum = mass × velocity	$p = mv$
gravitational potential energy = mass × gravitational field strength × height	$E_p = mgh$
power = $\dfrac{\text{work done}}{\text{time}}$	$P = \dfrac{W}{t}$
efficiency = $\dfrac{\text{useful power output}}{\text{total power input}}$	
charge flow = current × time	$Q = It$
power = potential difference × current	$P = VI$
energy transferred = power × time	$E = Pt$
density = $\dfrac{\text{mass}}{\text{volume}}$	$\rho = \dfrac{m}{V}$
work done = force × distance (along the line of action of the force)	$W = Fs$
distance travelled = speed × time	$s = vt$
resultant force = mass × acceleration	$F = ma$
kinetic energy = 0.5 × mass × (speed)²	$E_k = \dfrac{1}{2}mv^2$
power = $\dfrac{\text{energy transferred}}{\text{time}}$	$P = \dfrac{E}{t}$
efficiency = $\dfrac{\text{useful output energy transfer}}{\text{total input energy transfer}}$	
wave speed = frequency × wavelength	$v = f\lambda$
potential difference = current × resistance	$V = IR$
power = current² × resistance	$P = I^2R$
energy transferred = charge flow × potential difference	$E = QV$
pressure = $\dfrac{\text{force normal to a surface}}{\text{area of that surface}}$	$p = \dfrac{F}{A}$
moment of a force = force × distance (normal to direction of force)	$M = Fd$

You should be able to select and apply the following equations from the Physics equation sheet.

Word equation	Symbol equation
(final velocity)^2 − (initial velocity)^2 = 2 × acceleration × distance	$v^2 - u^2 = 2as$
elastic potential energy = 0.5 × spring constant × extension^2	$E_e = \dfrac{1}{2}ke^2$
period = $\dfrac{1}{\text{frequency}}$	
(H) force on a conductor (at right angles to a magnetic field) carrying a current = magnetic flux density × current × length	$F = BIl$
change in thermal energy = mass × specific heat capacity × temperature change	$\Delta E = mc\Delta\theta$
thermal energy for a change of state = mass × specific latent heat	$E = mL$
(H) potential difference across primary coil × current in primary coil = potential difference across secondary coil × current in secondary coil	$V_s I_s = V_p I_p$
(H) pressure due to a column of liquid = height of column × density of liquid × gravitational field strength	$p = h\rho g$
(H) $\dfrac{\text{potential difference across primary coil}}{\text{potential difference across secondary coil}}$ $= \dfrac{\text{number of turns in primary coil}}{\text{number of turns in secondary coil}}$	$\dfrac{V_p}{V_s} = \dfrac{n_p}{n_s}$
For gases: pressure × volume = constant	$pV = \text{constant}$
(H) force = $\dfrac{\text{change in momentum}}{\text{time taken}}$	$F = \dfrac{m\Delta v}{\Delta t}$
magnification = $\dfrac{\text{image height}}{\text{object height}}$	

Notes – 1 Specific heat capacity

Make notes on the practical you carried out.

_____

_____

_____

_____

_____

_____

Hint

Make notes on:
- your method
- safety precautions
- sources of error
- possible improvements
- the function of equipment
- how to make accurate measurements.

_____

_____

_____

_____

_____

_____

_____

_____

_____

_____

_____

_____

_____

_____

_____

Tip

You could use this space to:
- draw a diagram of the circuit and equipment used to measure the specific heat capacity of a block
- write an equation linking energy transferred, mass, temperature change, and specific heat capacity.

Notes – 2 Thermal insulation

Make notes on the practical you carried out.

_____

_____

_____

_____

_____

_____

_____

Hint

Make notes on:
- your method
- safety precautions
- sources of error
- possible improvements
- the function of equipment
- how to make accurate measurements.

_____

_____

_____

_____

_____

_____

_____

_____

_____

_____

_____

_____

_____

_____

Tip

You could use this space to:
- draw a sketch graph of a cooling curve
- write an equation linking rate of temperature change, time, and temperature change.

Notes – 3 Resistance

Make notes on the practical you carried out.

_____

_____

_____

_____

_____

_____

_____

Hint

Make notes on:
- your method
- safety precautions
- sources of error
- possible improvements
- the function of equipment
- how to make accurate
  measurements.

_____

_____

_____

_____

_____

_____

_____

_____

_____

_____

_____

_____

_____

Tip

You could use this space to:
- draw circuit diagrams of resistors in series and in parallel
- write an equation for the total resistance of three resistors in series
- sketch a diagram of resistance against length of wire.

Notes – 4 *I–V* characteristics

Make notes on the practical you carried out.

_____

_____

_____

_____

_____

_____

_____

Hint

Make notes on:
- your method
- safety precautions
- sources of error
- possible improvements
- the function of equipment
- how to make accurate measurements.

_____

_____

_____

_____

_____

_____

_____

_____

_____

_____

_____

_____

_____

_____

Tip

You could use this space to:
- draw circuit symbols for a diode, a thermistor, a filament lamp, and a variable resistor
- sketch *I–V* characteristics for a diode, a resistor, and a filament lamp.

Notes – 5 Density

Make notes on the practical you carried out.

_____

_____

_____

_____

_____

_____

Hint

Make notes on:
- your method
- safety precautions
- sources of error
- possible improvements
- the function of equipment
- how to make accurate
  measurements.

_____

_____

_____

_____

_____

_____

_____

_____

_____

_____

_____

_____

_____

_____

Tip

You could use this space to:
- write the equation that links density, mass, and volume
- sketch a labelled diagram showing a displacement can being used to
  measure the volume of an object.

Notes – 6 Force and extension

Make notes on the practical you carried out.

_____

_____

_____

_____

_____

_____

_____

Hint

Make notes on:
- your method
- safety precautions
- sources of error
- possible improvements
- the function of equipment
- how to make accurate measurements.

_____

_____

_____

_____

_____

_____

_____

_____

_____

_____

_____

_____

_____

_____

Tip

You could use this space to write the equations linking:
- force, spring constant, and extension
- weight, mass, and gravitational field strength.
You could also sketch a graph of force vs extension for a spring.

Notes – 7 Acceleration

Make notes on the practical you carried out.

_____

_____

_____

_____

_____

_____

_____

Hint

Make notes on:
- your method
- safety precautions
- sources of error
- possible improvements
- the function of equipment
- how to make accurate measurements.

_____

_____

_____

_____

_____

_____

_____

_____

_____

_____

_____

_____

_____

_____

Tip

You could use this space to:
- write the equation linking force, mass, and acceleration
- sketch a graph of acceleration against force.

Notes – 8 Waves

Make notes on the practical you carried out.

_____

_____

_____

_____

_____

_____

_____

Hint

Make notes on:
- your method
- safety precautions
- sources of error
- possible improvements
- the function of equipment
- how to make accurate measurements.

_____

_____

_____

_____

_____

_____

_____

_____

_____

_____

_____

_____

_____

_____

_____

Tip

You could use this space to:
- write equations for wave speed and frequency
- draw a labelled diagram of the equipment used to investigate waves on a string.

Notes – 9 Light

Make notes on the practical you carried out.

_____

_____

_____

_____

_____

_____

Hint

Make notes on:
- your method
- safety precautions
- sources of error
- possible improvements
- the function of equipment
- how to make accurate measurements.

_____

_____

_____

_____

_____

_____

_____

_____

_____

_____

_____

_____

_____

_____

Tip

You could use this space to draw labelled ray diagrams showing:
- a reflected ray
- a refracted ray.

Notes – 10 Radiation and absorption

Make notes on the practical you carried out.

_____

_____

_____

_____

_____

_____

_____

_____

Hint

Make notes on:
- your method
- safety precautions
- sources of error
- possible improvements
- the function of equipment
- how to make accurate measurements.

_____

_____

_____

_____

_____

_____

_____

_____

_____

_____

_____

_____

_____

_____

Tip

You could use this space to sketch the equipment you used to investigate infrared radiation from different surfaces.

Notes

Notes

Notes

Notes

Notes

Notes

OXFORD
UNIVERSITY PRESS

Great Clarendon Street, Oxford, OX2 6DP, United Kingdom

Oxford University Press is a department of the University of Oxford.
It furthers the University's objective of excellence in research,
scholarship, and education by publishing worldwide. Oxford is a
registered trade mark of Oxford University Press in the UK and in
certain other countries

British Library Cataloguing in Publication Data
Data available

978 0 19 844490 9

10 9 8 7 6 5

Paper used in the production of this book is a natural, recyclable
product made from wood grown in sustainable forests.
The manufacturing process conforms to the environmental regulations
of the country of origin.

Printed and bound by CPI Group (UK) Ltd, Croydon, CR0 4YY

Acknowledgements

COVER: IAN CUMING/IKON IMAGES/SCIENCE PHOTO LIBRARY

Artwork by Aptara Inc.